BIOGRAPHY FROM
ANCIENT CIVILIZATIONS
LEGENDS, FOLKLORE, AND STORIES OF ANCIENT WORLDS

The Life and Times of

ALEXANDER THE GREAT

Mitchell Lane
PUBLISHERS

P.O. Box 196
Hockessin, Delaware 19707

BIOGRAPHY FROM ANCIENT CIVILIZATIONS
LEGENDS, FOLKLORE, AND STORIES OF ANCIENT WORLDS

Titles
in the Series

The Life and Times of:

Alexander the Great
Archimedes
Aristotle
Augustus Caesar
Buddha
Catherine the Great
Charlemagne
Cicero
Cleopatra
Confucius
Constantine
Genghis Khan
Hammurabi
Herodotus
Hippocrates
Homer
Joan of Arc
Julius Caesar
King Arthur
Marco Polo
Moses
Nero
Pericles
Plato
Rameses the Great
Socrates

BIOGRAPHY FROM
ANCIENT CIVILIZATIONS
LEGENDS, FOLKLORE, AND STORIES OF ANCIENT WORLDS

The Life and Times of

ALEXANDER THE GREAT

by John Bankston

Printing   3   4   5   6   7   8
Library of Congress Cataloging-in-Publication Data

Bankston, John, 1974–
     The life and times of Alexander the Great / John Bankston.
          p. cm. — (Biography from ancient civilizations)
     Includes bibliographical references and index.
     Contents: A small kingdom for a horse—Learning the rules of ruling—Teen general—The great liberator—End of the reign.
     ISBN 1-58415-283-4 (Library Bound)
     1. Alexander, the Great, 356–323 b.c.—Juvenile literature. 2. Greece—History—Macedonian Expansion, 359–323 b.c.—Juvenile literature. 3. Generals—Greece—Biography—Juvenile literature. [1. Alexander, the Great, 356–323 b.c. 2. Kings, queens, rulers, etc. 3. Generals. 4. Greece—History—Macedonian Expansion, 359–323 b.c.] I. Title. II. Series.
     DF234 .B33 2004
     938'.07'092—dc22   2003024043

J-B
ALEXANDER
370-0369

ABOUT THE AUTHOR: Born in Boston, Massachusetts, John Bankston began publishing articles in newspapers and magazines while still a teenager. Since then, he has written over two hundred articles, and contributed chapters to books such as *Crimes of Passion*, and *Death Row 2000*, which have been sold in bookstores across the world. He was written numerous biographies for young adults, including Eminem and Nelly (Mitchell Lane). He currently lives in Portland, Oregon.

PHOTO CREDITS: Cover, title page, half-title page, pp. 10, 13, 19, 26, 34—Hulton Archive/Getty Images; p. 6—Superstock; pp. 15, 36—Giraudon/Art Resource, NY; p. 29 Photo Researchers; p. 41—Bettmann/CORBIS.

PUBLISHER'S NOTE: This story is based on the author's extensive research, which he believes to be accurate. Documentation of such research is contained on page 47.

The internet sites referenced herein were active as of the publication date. Due to the fleeting nature of some web sites, we cannot guarantee they will all be active when you are reading this book.

BIOGRAPHY FROM ANCIENT CIVILIZATIONS
LEGENDS, FOLKLORE, AND STORIES OF ANCIENT WORLDS

The Life and Times of

ALEXANDER THE GREAT

*For Your Information

An illustration of Alexander III with his horse, Bucephalus. Alexander was the first person to successfully tame Bucephalus. The horse continually threw other horsemen who had tried to ride him.

CHAPTER
ONE

A SMALL KINGDOM FOR A HORSE

No one could ride Bucephalus. The eight-year-old horse had bucked and thrown any rider who tried. That didn't matter to Alexander. The boy, who was also eight years old, had a deal to make.

He'd watched as his father, King Philip II, tried to get on Bucephalus. When the horse wouldn't let him, Philip demanded that his grooms get rid of it.

According to the writer Plutarch, Alexander spoke up. "What a horse they are losing, just because they don't know the best way to handle him, or if they do they dare not try."

Alexander's father was amused. "Do you presume to criticize those who are older than you, as if you know more and could do better?"[1]

Alexander replied that he was sure he could, but if he failed he'd pay what the horse cost. If he succeeded, the horse should be his.

The bet was on.

Alexander confidently approached Bucephalus. He had an idea. Watching earlier, he'd seen the horse rear up when it saw its shadow. Taking hold of the animal's bridle, he turned it toward the sun. Then the boy dropped his cloak on the ground and climbed upon the horse.

Chapter ONE

The crowd grew as Alexander galloped away. When he'd gone a short distance, he turned the horse around and rode straight toward his father and his groomsmen. He halted a few feet from Philip, raising a small cloud of dust. The group of observers broke into loud applause; his father clapped the hardest.

"O my son," Plutarch recorded him as saying, "find yourself a kingdom equal to and worthy of your ambitions, for Macedonia is too little for you."[2]

Philip's words predicted the future. Alexander would find a larger kingdom. In fact, he'd find many of them, and he'd conquer them all. The corner of Greece that Philip ruled was a small slice of land compared to the area Alexander would one day control.

Alexander would lead soldiers from his perch upon the horse he'd saved. Atop Bucephalus, he'd command the largest army the world had known. He'd rule a kingdom that stretched across two continents. Before he was 30 he'd be the richest man on the planet. Alexander would know love, he'd know loss, but he'd never know an end to his ambitions. Only his death ended his conquest.

Today, over two thousand years later, generals still study Alexander's battle plans. Alexander left his mark on Greece, a country that could not hold on to the territory he won, a country that itself would later be conquered by Rome. Yet its best-known son would create dozens of cities, some bearing his name. These places would outlast both him and the Greek empire.

Manuscripts preserved at libraries he founded were used by historians, including the writer Plutarch, and today give us a record of his life.

Alexander was more than just a king. He embraced the cultures and even the religions of the countries he invaded. He spread democracy, established in Greece nearly two centuries before his birth. The principles of giving citizens the right to vote for their leaders was extended across Asia. In many ways Alexander was more of a liberator than a conqueror.

Plutarch
(A.D. 46–c. 120)

Kings and warriors often kept official historians in their employ. These biographers recorded their bosses' lives for all time. Alexander was both a king *and* a warrior, and he used Callisthenes as his official historian. However, in 327 B.C., Alexander suspected Callisthenes of treason and, depending on the source, either had him executed directly or had him thrown into prison, where he died of sickness several months later.

Not only did his biographer's writing cease, but whatever Callisthenes wrote disappeared. In the two-plus millennia since Alexander's reign, only fragments of writings from the time he was alive still exist. Yet modern readers are able to find out much about Alexander the Great, and Plutarch is one reason for this.

The work of Mestrius Plutarchus—known as Plutarch—offers a detailed picture of Alexander's life. A former priest at the temple of Apollo, Plutarch lived some four hundred years after Alexander. However, he was able to use manuscripts that do not exist today—including books written by Callisthenes, Chares, and Aristobulus.

Some historians today suspect Plutarch of exaggerating some of his stories, but two thousand years ago he had an answer for them, saying, "It is so hard to find out the truth of anything by looking at a record of the past. The process of time obscures the truth of former times, and even contemporaneous writers disguise and twist the truth."

Philip II was king of Macedonia and the father of Alexander the Great. He became the ruler of Macedonia, a highland region that lies to the north of Greece, after his two older brothers were killed.

CHAPTER TWO

LEARNING THE RULES OF RULING

The battle was over and the king was ready to take another wife. Philip II had come to power as the ruler of Macedonia after his two older brothers had been killed. The first one, Alexander II, had been assassinated by his mother's boyfriend just over a year after taking the throne; the other, Perdiccas III, was killed in battle soon after.

When Philip came to power in 359 B.C., he was 23 years old and he inherited a mess. Macedonia was just one of many city-states in Greece, but these regions didn't get along. Tribes from neighboring areas regularly attacked Macedonia. Although it was somewhat isolated and protected by a mountain range (which included Mount Olympus, the largest mountain in Greece), it still had to defend itself against other tribes who thought Macedonia was weak.

The citizens of Macedonia believed in the same gods and spoke the same language as the rest of Greece, but their Greek was flavored with a Doric accent typical of northerners. Most southern Greeks considered themselves superior to northerners, and therefore they looked down on Macedonians.

Although Macedonia was ruled by a king, the ruler wasn't always the previous king's oldest living son. Instead, kings were chosen by a group of elite soldiers who often argued for days about the selection. Sometimes the fights led to bloodshed, even mini-revolutions. Because the transfer of power was messy, neighboring tribes saw the confusion as an opportunity to attack. This is exactly what happened as Philip was becoming king.

Like the U.S. president, the king of Macedonia was also the commander in chief of the armed forces. Unlike our president, the king rode with his soldiers and led the military campaigns, leaving a trusted adviser behind while battles raged.

Philip spent a year training his army as the neighboring Illyrian tribes prepared to invade. During that year he also had his half brothers executed, men he believed were plotting to kill him in hopes of becoming king. Beginning in the spring of 358 B.C., Philip led his well-trained army in a successful invasion of Paeonia; defeated the Illyrian king, Bardylis; and invaded Thessaly to the north. He also attacked the city of Amphipolis, which while only a few miles from Macedonia's border was controlled by Athens.

It was a busy year.

In the fall of 357 B.C., Philip married Princess Polyxena Myrtale, renaming her Olympias, as was his right. The daughter of Epirus's King Neoptolemus, she was Philip's third wife. His first two wives had died without giving him a boy—and in ancient Greece, boys were prized and women were considered second-class citizens (among other things, they weren't allowed to vote).

Depending on the account, their son was born on either July 20 or July 26 in the year 356 B.C. He was named Alexander III after Philip's brother.

If Alexander didn't see his father much, there was a good reason. Philip was often out fighting battles, defending the borders of his city-state. As Alexander grew up, his father married at least six more women—several of whom gave him sons as well.

Alexander's firstborn status was not a guarantee to the throne.

Raised in an enormous palace in Pella, his upbringing fell mainly to his nurse, Lanice (or Lanike), whose sister was married to a military commander. Although Lanice was significant in Alexander's life, his mother also spent a great deal of time with him. She told him he would grow up to be a great leader. She told him that the Greek god Zeus was his real father. She told him a lot of things, and he almost always believed her.

Alexander's mother was a great follower of the Greek religion, which honored many gods. Her family believed the hero of Homer's *Iliad*,

This engraving shows Alexander and his mother, Olympias

Achilles, was a direct relative. A worshiper of Dionysus, the god of wine and good times, Olympias took part in religious ceremonies with other women and snakes. According to Plutarch, these reptiles "would lie concealed, then rear their heads and coil themselves around the wands and garlands of the women in order to terrify the men."[1] The writer also claims that it was a snake sharing their bed which ruined the marriage of Philip and Olympias.

Olympias may also have told her son he was the child of Zeus because she and Philip were getting along so poorly. The couple would have another child together—daughter Cleopatra—but Olympias hated that her husband had other wives and children. Plural marriages, in which a man has several wives, were common in Greece and indeed in much of the world at that time. The fact that it was an accepted practice in society, however, did not make it any more acceptable to Olympias. As far as she was concerned, she should be number one in her husband's affections.

Between his mother and his nurse, Alexander received so much attention and praise, he was hopelessly spoiled by the time he was ready to be formally educated.

Alexander was seven years old when Leonidas, a relative of Olympias, began to tutor him. The spoiling ended. Instead, as Plutarch relates, Alexander complained, "He used to come and look through my bedding boxes and clothing chests to see that my mother did not hide any luxuries for me."[2] Although Alexander hated his tutor's strictness, Leonidas gave him an early love for the arts—for poetry, sculpture, singing, and the theater. A harsh comment by Philip ended Alexander's public singing, but Alexander's support of the arts and artists never ceased.

For Alexander, reading Homer's *Iliad* was like reading a family history. He believed he was related to the hero Achilles and like him was the son of a mortal woman and a god. Quoting Homer, Alexander would often tell people, "Ever to be best and stand far above all others."

While he read about battles, he also endured rigorous military training conducted by Lysimachus, a member of his father's royal court. Under his tutelage, Alexander learned all about combat techniques, the use of weapons like javelins and lances, battle strategy, and horsemanship. The final skill was aptly demonstrated when young Alexander rode Bucephalus.

On Alexander's 13th birthday, his father had to make an important decision. Most teens from royal and well-to-do families were educated at the Athens Academy, the most respected high school in Greece. Unfortunately, Philip had so many enemies in that southern Greek city, he was afraid his son wouldn't live long enough to graduate.

Since Alexander couldn't go to the Athens Academy, the Athens Academy went to Alexander.

Alexander III was born to King Philip and Queen Olympias. From an early age Olympias told Alexander that the Greek God Zeus was his father.

Becoming a royal tutor was an enormous honor. Even the principal of the Athens Academy offered to quit his job to teach Alexander. Philip turned him down, selecting instead a teacher from the school who would become one of the most famous scholars in the world.

When he began teaching the teenage Alexander, Aristotle was in his forties. At that time the skinny philosopher's greatest claim to fame was being a student of the respected Plato, who'd died in 347 B.C. He was also a respected scientist from a family with a strong background in medicine. Arriving at the royal court, Aristotle moved into a large house, where he would also give Alexander his lessons. He taught Alexander subjects like botany (the study of plants) and zoology (the study of animals) along with medicine. However, the young man's education was designed for more than just increasing his knowledge— it was to prepare him to rule. There was no guarantee Alexander would become king, but he had to be ready if he were chosen. And so he learned law and politics, history and philosophy, all focused on the decisions he might have to make.

As Alexander studied, Philip faced growing conflicts along his borders. The Anti-Macedonian League was formed by rulers of Thebes and Byzantium to keep Philip's city-state from getting too much power. To Philip, the league's formation signified one thing: war was on the horizon.

King Philip would have to lead his men into battle against Byzantium. Someone would have to be left in charge of Macedonia. Philip decided to pick the man he trusted most: his firstborn son. Alexander was well trained and educated, but he was also only 16 years old. Many members of the royal court wondered if he was up to the job.

They were about to find out.

A God Among Men

FYI

For Your Info

Alexander grew up believing he was the child of a god. In ancient Greece, this wasn't the idle fantasy of a crazy man; it was part of an elaborate belief system handed down for centuries. The Greeks, unlike most religious followers today, worshiped many gods, and Alexander even adopted the gods of the countries he conquered into Greece's belief system.

The Greek gods were seen as a family, and Zeus, the king of the gods, fathered many of them. Zeus ruled the earth from his home atop Mount Olympus; Alexander believed Zeus was as real as Greece's highest mountain. Although Zeus was married to the goddess of marriage, Hera, he had many children with many wives, some mortal and some divine. One of his sons was Apollo, the god of light. Apollo's oracle at Delphi predicted the future, and both King Philip and Alexander III relied on the oracle's wisdom.

Olympias focused her worship on Zeus's youngest son, Dionysus, the god of wine. Worshiping this god included drinking great amounts of wine in order to escape from everyday cares. The wild events held in this god's name were legendary.

The gods of Greece influenced not only the Greeks, but also the Romans, who became the Greeks' eventual rulers. Romans adapted many of the qualities of the Greek gods and applied them to their own: Zeus became Jupiter, and Hera became Juno. However, they did not have a god like Apollo, so they just took him as their own, name and all.

King Philip arranged a deal with the Greek philosopher Aristotle to come to Macedonia and teach Alexander personally.

CHAPTER

THREE

TEEN GENERAL

Whenever power shifted in one of the Greek city-states, the other city-states took advantage. When a 16-year-old boy was left in charge of Macedonia in 340 B.C., revolts were inevitable.

Alexander had been appointed Regent of Macedonia. The title was more than just a sign of respect from his father; it also meant that King Philip saw the boy as next in line for the throne. For the first time, he was truly *Prince* Alexander.

Prince Alexander's military training was about to be put to the test. Tribes along Macedonia's border revolted, but, leading a superior force, Alexander quickly overwhelmed them. After the battle ended, Alexander commanded his soldiers to drive everyone out—the land was given to Macedonians loyal to the king. The young prince named the settlement Alexandropolis (the City of Alexander).

When Philip returned from his own success, he was overwhelmed with pride for his offspring. He promoted Alexander to general. Finally father and son had something they could enjoy together: warfare. Over the course of a year, the two led legions of well-trained soldiers as King Philip expanded his territory.

During one battle, Alexander again proved his value. Philip was wounded and unable to continue the fight. Falling to the ground, he pretended to be dead. His son protected him. Later the proud king refused to even acknowledge that Alexander had saved his life.

By the summer of 339 B.C., Philip was ready to take on the Anti-Macedonian League. The organization was gaining dangerous power as Athens and Thebes united with 10,000 private soldiers called mercenaries—men who'd fight for anyone as long as their price was met. The battle between the League and Macedonia peaked along a strip of land near the Cephisus River. The cavalry—or horse-mounted soldiers—from each side numbered 2,000, and Philip and his son commanded an infantry regiment numbering 30,000.

It was a huge army, but the Macedonians were outnumbered. The Thebes-Athens side had about 5,000 more men, and they were fighting on familiar ground.

However, the wily king had at least one good trick up his sleeve. He and his men pretended to fall back in retreat. The Athenians followed. Their Theban allies were left behind. Alexander made his move.

He led his army into the space between the Thebans and the Athenians, overwhelming the smaller, unprepared force. By then all the king's men had turned and marched toward the Athenians, their sharp pikes impaling their opponents.

The battle's conclusion demonstrated King Philip's cruelty and kindness. He rounded up the citizens of Thebes and sold them as slaves. But he also forged a peace pact with the Athenians, returning both the bodies of the dead and their prisoners of war.

By the fall, the Greek city-states that once opposed Philip's rule elected him Supreme Commander of the Greek Forces. The new title applied to all of Philip's male offspring as well. As the oldest, Alexander was certain he was in line for the throne.

By 337 B.C., all of that changed.

Philip fell in love that year and married Attalus's niece, a teenager named Cleopatra. Philip renamed her Eurydice. None of his previous marriages threatened Alexander and his mother like this one: Philip had named his new bride after his own mother. Then at the wedding party, as Plutarch reports, Attalus proclaimed that everyone should pray that his niece produce "a legitimate heir."[1]

It was a clear insult to Alexander. He stood up and flung his cup at Attalus. Then Alexander turned and insulted his father, who responded by drawing his sword and advancing on his son.

The king was too drunk to do any damage. Embarrassingly, he tripped and fell facedown. "Look at him," Alexander is quoted as saying, "the man is preparing to cross from Europe to Asia and he can't get from one table to another."[2]

Then Alexander left. He took his mother to her brother, King Alexander of Epirus, and rode to Illyria. The choice was deliberate: The town had once revolted against Philip's rule. By going there, the prince showed he might be considering a rebellion of his own.

With his angry wife at one end of the country and a rebellious son at the other, Philip couldn't leave. His battle plans for Persia were frozen. Eventually a mutual friend helped father and son make up, but although Alexander returned to Macedonia, there was still hostility between the two.

When Philip sent a group of soldiers into Asia Minor, he let General Parmenio and Attalus (who was also the general's son-in-law) lead them. It was an enormous slight to Alexander.

Philip's days of disrespecting Alexander were numbered.

In the summer of 336 B.C., Philip and his young bride Eurydice had a son. He named the boy Caranus after the founder of his royal dynasty. There could be no clearer signal. Philip saw his new son as next in line to the throne.

Worse, that summer Philip celebrated his daughter Cleopatra's marriage to King Alexander of Epirus. By marrying his daughter to his wife's brother, Philip strengthened the alliance between his family and Olympias's family, repairing any political damage caused by his unraveling marriage to Olympias.

During the wedding celebration in Agae, a statue of Philip was set to follow a dozen statues of Greek gods. The parade didn't happen. At the last moment, King Philip changed his plans to enter the arena beside his son and new brother-in-law: the Alexanders. Instead, he would go in alone. Awaiting his entrance, standing beside bodyguard Pausanias, the king was unprepared when the man paid to protect him instead pulled a dagger and with a single thrust jabbed it between Philip's ribs.

The king was dead before he hit the ground.

The bodyguard fled on foot, running toward horses waiting for him outside the city. He never made it. Philip's other bodyguards caught and killed him.

Chaos erupted. Revolts grew around Macedonia. The king's power over the border tribes disappeared with his last breath. But son Alexander was ready.

Few questioned who would be the next king of Macedonia. Alexander had proved himself in battle. The city-state needed a strong soldier to lead them. At 20 years old, Alexander became King Alexander III, with the power of Macedonia's armies behind him. His first duty as king was to find the men who'd helped kill his father.

The man who murdered King Philip had horses waiting for him, and an escape route. Such organization suggested a conspiracy—that more than one person had plotted to kill the king.

Alexander rounded up the usual suspects—people who had the most to gain by the king's death. Of course some have wondered if that person was Olympias herself, who wanted to see her son as king and who hated Philip. The Macedonian Assembly, which was like a senate, ruled that the plotters were two of Aeropus's sons and Attalus himself. Attalus was killed resisting arrest, and the other two were executed. Even the infant Caranus was killed for treason.

The women members of the family were excluded from punishment, except for Eurydice. Olympias had the young bride arrested and brought in chains to her home. There she took care of the woman personally. Most accounts report that she burned Eurydice alive.

Alexander had resolved his father's murder. He'd seen him buried in an elaborate gold chest, which also held his crown and other royal jewels (all of which were unearthed late in the 20th century).

Now, Alexander was ready for war.

His first goal was to deal with the rebellion. Maybe cities like Thessaly, Argos, and Sparta counted on the new king to be too overwhelmed by his new job to deal with the revolution. They counted wrong.

Instead, Alexander massed his army into a tight formation and drove them into revolting cites, cities that were unprepared for the sheer number of opponents. Most surrendered with little bloodshed.

Afterward Alexander called a meeting of the Hellenic League. They elected him Supreme Commander of the Greek Forces and promised to back him in a campaign against hated Persia.

In the early months of 335 B.C., Alexander began to hone his army. His father had done most of the training already.

King Philip had inherited a disorganized, poorly equipped military and turned it into the most powerful army in Greece. He did this by constant practice, running military drills and teaching his men to move in regimented formation. He doubled the infantry to over 34,000 and more than tripled the cavalry to 3,000.

More than the men, more than the horses, the best attack weapon Alexander inherited from his father was the Macedonian phalanx. Each phalanx consisted of 256 men in rows of 16 wide by columns 16 deep. Wielding pikes—very long wooden poles with an iron spear at the end—the phalanx would march forward, their shields raised in protection. Their pikes would impale anything and everything that got in their way. On level ground the Macedonian phalanx was virtually unstoppable.

Alexander and his men were ready for battle by the spring of 335 B.C. Leaving his trusted deputy, Antipater, in charge of Macedonia, the new king led his well-trained forces into combat.

Their first enemies came from within Greece. Small tribes along the border had continued to revolt against Macedonia's rule. Alexander took care of them quickly.

About to fight the Thracians, he learned that most of them had taken refuge on higher ground. In combat, the side with the height advantage often wins. From atop Mount Haemus, the Thracians had lined up wagons. They planned to release these, hoping they'd run over the Macedonians.

Alexander had spies. Learning of their plans, he had his men lie down in a narrow area and interlock their shields. The soldiers were like turtles protected by their shells. The wagons passed over without effect, and with them the Thracians' best defense. In the battle that followed, Alexander lost few men, but 1,500 of his opponents lay dead.

Alexander's army was fortunate to have a leader trained by Aristotle, a man with a strong background in medicine. Alexander employed the best doctors and often used what he'd learned as a teenager on the battlefield.

The Triballains faced a similar outcome as the Thracians—3,000 dead to just 51 from Alexander's army. At the northern border, Alexander's army defeated a superior force by filling their tents with hay and using these to float across the Ister River at night. By first light the enemy had been surprised and defeated.

There were other battles, but they all had the same conclusion: victory for Alexander.

Medical Miracles

Until the 20th century, with its emphasis on antibiotics and other disease-fighting medicines, more soldiers died from illnesses than injuries. Alexander's men usually suffered fewer losses than the armies they faced, but on the journeys to the battlefield, they were vulnerable to unfamiliar diseases native to the lands they invaded. Diseases such as malaria and cholera killed more soldiers than arrows and spears.

They were lucky to have Alexander as a leader. He'd been educated by a man of medicine, and he valued doctors greatly. He made regular use of herbs such as hellebore, a white flower that produced a healing and pain-reducing drug. Alexander employed the best doctors, both from Macedonia and from the countries he conquered. These doctors were invaluable in providing information about local illnesses and their best treatment.

Unfortunately, Alexander's doctors also relied on a method called bleeding. This ancient practice, which survived into the 19th century, involved a doctor slicing into a patient in hopes that whatever was making him sick would flow out with the blood. This dangerous technique killed as many as it "cured."

Alexander's most modern idea was his belief that exercise and physical training promoted health. He felt that a strong body was a soldier's best weapon. This isn't surprising: Greece, after all, gave the world the Olympics.

DARIVS.

King Darius ruled the Persian empire after Cyrus. During his reign, the Greeks and the Persians met in conflict, which ended with the Persians' defeat at Marathon.

CHAPTER FOUR

THE GREAT LIBERATOR

To the east awaited Alexander's greatest enemy: King Darius of Persia. The 50-year-old leader was considered by some later writers to be a poor military leader, but he proved his cunning by bringing the fight to Alexander.

Instead of leading troops into Greece, Darius paid Demosthenes to give a speech at the Athenian Assembly. He told the assembly that Alexander and all of his men had been killed in battle.

The lie worked. Thebes and Athens joined with Persia, hoping to take over Macedonia once and for all. With their combined force, Demosthenes' announcement might not have been a lie after all.

It might have been a prophecy.

Alexander's men were worn out. Encamped in Pelium, the young king learned of the revolt by messenger. Thebes lay 250 miles north. There was no choice. They had to move before Macedonia was attacked.

Saddling up Bucephalus, he made the trek in less than two weeks. Even by modern standards, moving such a large army that distance in so short a period of time is a challenge. In 335 B.C. it was unheard of.

Just a few weeks before, the Thebans and Athenians had made him Supreme Commander of the Greek Forces. Now, assuming him dead, they were about to attack his birthplace.

Fighting back the rage he felt at the betrayal, once he reached the walls of Thebes, Alexander still offered peace. He wanted to deal with the rebellion's leaders personally. Getting an offer from a man they'd assumed was dead must have been a shock, but they still turned him down.

Having blocked the main road from Athens (along with potential Athenian reinforcements), the Macedonian army broke through the Theban defenses. Before it was over, 6,000 Theban soldiers were killed, while 20,000 citizens were captured and sold as slaves.

And then, just as his father had, Alexander forgave Athens.

Only traitorous Persia remained.

Alexander's army rested and trained before returning to the battle road in early 334 B.C. Alexander left the continent of Europe for Asia; he would never return home. He would also never see Olympias again. She was the mother of the king but she had no power—a reality she resented for the rest of her life.

Her son was the first person off the ship at Asia Minor, and, hurling a spear into the moist sand, he claimed the area as part of his kingdom.

Alexander commanded former enemies—citizens of city-states that had revolted against him rode beside Macedonian warriors. All told he commanded a force of over 40,000 infantrymen and 6,000 cavalry. It was an impressive army.

Reaching Troy, Alexander offered sacrifices to the gods and visited the tomb of Achilles, his supposed ancestor. The ritual was one more step toward immortality. Alexander was beginning to believe what his mother had told him—that he was related to gods, making him unstoppable and invincible.

Soon the men he commanded would believe it as well.

In May of 334 B.C., his army reached the Granicus River. On the other side, thousands of Persians, including a cavalry force of over 20,000, were girded for battle. Cloaked by darkness, Alexander set General Parmenio on the left flank and the general's son Philotas on the right. The king rode up between the two forces, hidden by the night, then tread lightly through a shallow stretch of the river.

The Battle of Granicus is depicted here in this painting by Philoxenos.

The Persians responded by focusing on the flanks, separating their men as Alexander's forces poured through their unprotected center. The Persians didn't realize they were slowly being surrounded. Alexander's army squeezed tight like a fist; in its wake 20,000 Persians lay dead or dying alongside the corpses of 15,000 mercenaries.

News of the victory would precede Alexander's army. He led his men south through Asia Minor, into open arms and gratitude. Under Darius's rule the citizens had few rights; they saw Alexander as a liberator bringing democracy to their land.

Indeed, he even let the cities he entered keep their local laws and leaders while eliminating the taxes they paid to the crown.

Although small battles sprang up here and there, with every mile Alexander gained supporters. By late 334 B.C., it was safe to give all the newly married soldiers the winter off. He sent them home to their wives with orders to return in the spring.

Early the next year he reached the town of Gordium in Phrygia, where he famously untied the Gordian knot. This crazy construction of coils had challenged thousands. According to legend, any man who unraveled the puzzle could rule the land. Alexander approached the knot, looked at it for a moment, and then drew his sword and sliced it in two. Problem solved!

Meanwhile, King Darius may have hoped geography would preserve his rule. Unfortunately for him, the Taurus Mountains slowed but didn't stop Alexander's advance. The treacherous Cilician Gates didn't stop him either. This natural gap in the mountains allowed men to move through only four abreast—a dangerous situation for an army. It was the perfect place for a Persian attack. Instead, again moving at night, Alexander's men surprised the few guards watching the pass. The guards fled in terror rather than fight his army.

Opposing armies and mountains couldn't stop him, but illness did. In September, Alexander began running such a high fever that not only did he have to stop his march, for a while his personal physicians feared the leader was dying. He wasn't, but he needed time to get better.

King Darius assumed his opponent was too afraid to fight.

The Persian king assembled an enormous force—over 600,000 men—preparing for battle along the flat plains of Syria. It was an ideal place for a superior army. No amount of combat skill could save Alexander. Even with recent reinforcements, he commanded less than 10 percent of the men Darius did.

If King Darius had waited, victory might well have been his. But he did not wait.

Instead, he impatiently drove his men out of the safe plains toward Cilicia, where the guards had reported Alexander's intrusion. The Persians were too late. Alexander had left and was traveling in the opposite direction, toward Syria. The armies actually passed each other, divided only by the Amanus Mountains.

The Persian army reached a field hospital Alexander had set up. Filled with Greek wounded, King Darius showed his ruthlessness by ordering the execution of the defenseless soldiers. Only a few survived the bloodshed. Those that did made their way in boats across the Bay of Issus.

The battle became personal. Persia had once invaded Greece, reason enough for the country's anger toward them. Now the king had killed wounded soldiers. It didn't matter that Alexander might have done the same thing. He was enraged and swore revenge.

With first light Alexander led his army toward a thin strip of land bounded by the Mediterranean Sea on one side, the Amanus Mountains on the other. The move limited Darius's advantage of having so many men. Despite their superior numbers, only a few of them could mass along the tiny beach. Worse, the soldiers in the cavalry could barely move because the animals' hooves sank into the moist sand.

It was the perfect place to demonstrate the Macedonian phalanx attack.

When Darius's forces arrived, Alexander was dug in and ready. The Persian king lined 10,000 of his best cavalry along the shoreline.

The opposing armies were divided by the Payas River, which flowed from the nearby mountains, cut along the beach, and terminated at the sea. Lined up on one bank were the skilled archers of Darius's army. Facing them was the Macedonian army, led by Alexander astride Bucephalus, who charged straight toward them. Defending a poorly trained and unmotivated infantry force made up of mainly mercenaries, the Persian archers turned and crashed right into their comrades.

There was chaos.

As the archers' defense collapsed, Alexander galloped Bucephalus straight at the center of the Persian army. With his sword raised high above his head, looking like the bronze god many thought he was, the young king moved quickly through the front lines of the Persian army and toward their king.

Darius was stunned. Alexander seemed unconcerned by his enemy's superior forces. His men didn't seem to care if they lived or died.

They seemed unbeatable.

Instead of fighting, Darius turned his horse around and fled. The rest of his men followed; the battle ended. The king left behind both a tent full of treasure and female members of his family. Alexander promised the women, including Darius's wife, mother, and several daughters, that no harm would come to them and that they'd be treated as a royal family.

Again Alexander refused to pursue Darius. Instead he enjoyed quiet victories through territory that had belonged to Persia. Whole villages greeted him as a liberator. By late 333 B.C., Alexander had reached the island city of Tyre, which lay 800 yards off the coast of Palestine in the Mediterranean. Alexander proved he was willing to flaunt his power regardless of the consequences. He announced by messenger his intention to offer a sacrifice to Heracles. According to Plutarch, Alexander believed Heracles was another one of his ancestors. Better known today by his Latin name Hercules, the demi-god of strength was an appropriate hero for Alexander. Unfortunately, only Tyrian kings were allowed to offer sacrifices to him. Letting Alexander do so would announce that he was their new ruler.

Leaders in Tyre refused to allow this.

The war began.

The challenge to Alexander's army seemed insurmountable. Lying protected in the shadow of 150-foot walls, Tyre seemed impervious to attack. Before a boat could approach its shoreline, arrows would rain down on it. Before a man could scale its walls, roasting hot sand would be dropped on his head.

King Alexander had an idea. He brought in an engineer named Diades who drew the plans, and, relying on nearby materials—stone walls from a ruined city, trees from a neighboring forest—the Macedonians began to build a causeway. This raised road would run across the water right to the Tyrian walls.

Helped by locals, the causeway's construction progressed quickly until it was 150 yards from the island. The Tyrians sent out ships ready for battle. Again, Alexander was prepared. He widened the causeway and erected 150-foot-tall catapults, which could hurl large stones into any boats that tried to attack.

Extending the causeway to Tyre was just one challenge. Defended by catapults and accompanied by the Macedonian fleet, the allied Phoenicians, and other villages that vowed loyalty to Alexander, the army was formidable. Still, the Tyrians had the walls and the hot sand, which sent the screaming wounded plunging into the ocean below. They'd rather drown than suffer from the burns. Meanwhile Tyrian arrows picked off any climbers the hot sand missed. Suddenly the battle looked like a bloody tie.

Alexander's courage won the day. Bringing in ships from the Cypriot and Phoenician navies, he directed them to attack and draw the fire of the Tyrians. Then he led his men to a less defended area and scaled the walls. When the king breached the Tyrians' defenses, they knew the war was over.

The battle was finished, but the dying continued.

In the war, 6,000 Tyrians were killed, and afterward 30,000 villagers were enslaved. However, the worst treatment came for some 2,000 surviving Tyrian fighters. The men were brought out and crucified along the shoreline.

It was a gruesome message to any who saw it. Defying Alexander brought severe punishment.

With the capture of Tyre, Macedonia now had a naval base. Darius was still out there, but Alexander was in no hurry to catch him. He traveled throughout Egypt, where Darius's rule was hated and Alexander was welcomed as a pharaoh, a king. While there he developed a city near Lake Mareotis, where he believed the harbor would be perfect for trade by ship. He drew an outline of the proposed city and named it Alexandria, one of 70 cities he would develop. The city would grow prosperous, its library world-famous for its Greek texts.

Alexander came across Darius' mother, wife, and others left behind after the Battle of Issus.

Then, despite a war to be won and land to be seized, Alexander's conquest again took a backseat to his other interests.

Later in 332 B.C., along with a few of his men, Alexander traveled across Egypt's western desert to visit the oracle of Amun. Alexander believed Amun to be like the god Zeus, the deity he believed to be his father.

Alexander told the priests this, and some accounts even claim he told them how to answer his questions. What answer they gave is unknown. But his earthly father once misinterpreted the predictions of the oracle of Delphi. King Philip had sent representatives to ask the priestess whether or not he'd conquer the Persian king. As oracle, the priestess told him, "The sacrificer awaits."[1]

There were many sacrifices in Alexander's future, but for him it was Darius who awaited. When Darius offered ransom money for the family members he had abandoned, Alexander refused. When he gave Alexander his permission to marry his daughter, Alexander told the king he didn't need his permission. If he wanted her, he'd have her.

King Alexander's replies enraged King Darius. He was hungry for blood. Blood is exactly what he got.

Alexandria

Although it may not have been his intention, Alexander's history became Alexandria's history. After Alexander's death in Babylon, the king's half brother Ptolemy stole his body and brought it back to the city Alexander had founded. Warfare followed the great King Alexander's death, and it took five decades before stable dynasties, including Ptolemy's, began to rule Egypt. It would be the Ptolemy clan that would pour much of their available wealth into Alexandria, making it one of the most advanced cities in the ancient world.

Alexandria, Greece

As part of the cultural improvement, Ptolemy founded the Museum and Library at Alexandria. The Egyptian went to great lengths to insure that the library had the best of everything. It is said that any ship entering Alexandria's harbor was thoroughly searched, and any books discovered on board were confiscated. The books were then brought to the library and copied; the originals were kept, and the owners received the copies. One of the Seven Wonders of the Ancient World, the library at Alexandria eventually accumulated an astonishing 700,000 volumes, including handwritten works by Homer, Aristotle, and Plato, and important books by Egyptian authors and writers from the rest of the known world.

Biographies of Alexander were borrowed from the library at Alexandria by writers such as Plutarch. The library's preservation of Greek history was one reason many books, including the New Testament of the Bible, were written in Greek. Even though most people spoke another language, Greek was the language of scholars and authors.

No one knows exactly when or how the library was destroyed. Many have believed it was burned. At any event, the city was victim to numerous riots, which eventually wrecked the contents of one of Alexander's great legacies.

Alexander confronted Darius again at the Battle of Gaugemela. Alexander was very confident as the battle neared. His victories at Granicus, Issus, and Tyre made his men believe that he was invincible.

CHAPTER
FIVE

END OF THE REIGN

It was the battle Darius and Alexander had been waiting for. In Gaugamela, Assyria, on October 1, 331 B.C., Alexander told his troops that this was the final conflict, the war for all of Asia. His soldiers— some 40,000 infantry and 7,000 cavalry—had crossed hundreds of miles of arid desert, suffering in full armor beneath the summer heat.

Not far away, King Darius was prepared. He had over 100,000 infantry and 40,000 cavalry at his command. Alexander's men would face elephants armored and ready for combat and chariots with blades attached to their wheels. But the Macedonians had prevailed against worse odds.

They were ready.

In the center of Alexander's army was the Macedonian phalanx. Alexander needed to find a weakness in the Persian battle lines. Then he could drive his best weapon right through it. Alexander's opening came quickly. He changed horses, climbing onto the well-traveled back of the aging Bucephalus.

Astride his familiar horse, Alexander could see King Darius across the way. He galloped toward him, parting a weak section in the Persian defenses, his men following close behind. With a mighty throw he hurled a spear straight at the king. It missed Darius and pierced his unfortunate charioteer. Darius took the reins from the dead man and fled for his life.

Their leader's cowardice inspired his men to retreat as well. The battle was over almost before it began, but again Darius was free.

Alexander could have followed the frightened king across the treacherous Taurus Mountains, but instead he decided to enjoy some of the property he now commanded. Darius's retreat left Alexander king of all Asia, and he and his men strode confidently into Babylon (modern-day Iraq.) The king settled into the luxurious 600-room palace of Nebuchadrezzar.

Again Alexander honored the native gods and even allowed once outlawed religious practices to flourish. This helped him and his men gain the support of their new subjects. Unfortunately, the support of his own men was diminishing. Many of Alexander's top generals resented the way he adopted the customs of the people he commanded, taking on the qualities of Persian royalty, including wearing their clothes. Most distasteful to the men he commanded was his instituting the Persian custom of obeisance, a formal bow.

Meanwhile, there were other battles, including one at Persepolis in which Alexander's men suffered heavy losses. By 330 B.C., Alexander learned that Darius and his men were camped 400 miles away, near Bactra in Persia. Leading his soldiers across what is today the Iranian desert just west of present-day Tehran, the army trekked the distance in an astonishing 11 days.

Exhausted, the group rested. Meanwhile, Darius was moving toward what is now Afghanistan.

And then Alexander learned some promising news. Many of King Darius's men had deserted. His cousin Bessus was appointed new leader. Darius was under arrest. The night he learned this, Alexander brought together 500 of his best horsemen, and the group rode until dawn. The light revealed a cloud of dust in the distance: Darius (bound in golden chains) and his men. Darius's captors wanted to flee, but the once great Persian king refused to leave.

Darius wanted to stay and fight. His captors didn't think this was a very good idea—they made their point with the end of a javelin. Under Bessus's orders, they stabbed Darius and fled into the sands, leaving their former king to bleed in the desert. Although Alexander's men found Darius shortly before he died, Alexander never had a chance to say a word to his rival.

Still, Alexander gave the man a noble burial.

In 328 B.C., Alexander won a battle against Bactria, part of the Persian Empire, and courted a Bactrian nobleman's daughter, Roxane. The two were married in a local ceremony.

War made victorious soldiers rich. Alexander's men were permitted to keep all they could carry. When they retired, they would be able to live comfortable lives from the treasure they'd taken; if they died, their families were well taken care of.

The treasure made the soldiers lazy. They became less motivated to train and practice. Alexander believed a soldier's most important piece of equipment was his body; in his spare time the king hunted lions to stay in shape. Plutarch quoted the king telling his men, "Haven't you learned yet that the honor and perfection of our victory consists in avoiding the vices that have made our enemies so easy to beat?"[1]

Maybe his men were tired of his demands or upset by his adoption of Persian customs. In 327 B.C. a number of his leaders, including his official historian Callisthenes, were involved in a plot to overthrow him. Alexander learned of the conspiracy and had them executed.

By then there was little to motivate his men for their next conquest: India. Early one morning, Alexander watched as the wagons were loaded, the horses struggling with the weight of their cargo. There was no way they could make the journey all the way to India. Was this the same army that had crossed deserts, that had made a

400-mile march in less than two weeks? Burn it all, Alexander commanded. He set fire to the wagons, including his own, torching the royal clothing he'd worn and some of his treasure.

His trick worked. Relieved of their cargo, the men felt like warriors again. They were ready to fight.

The beginning of the war against India could not have gone better. King Taxiles had no interest in taking on the great Alexander. Instead he started a different type of battle—a war to see who could give the other the most treasure!

Only King Porus, who controlled a small part of India, presented an obstacle. A huge man, he rode an elephant like it was a horse. Although he fought strongly, he too was defeated. Alexander's greatest loss came in that battle, as his trusty horse, Bucephalus, died from wounds endured in that combat. Still, instead of having King Porus killed, Alexander expanded the king's territory.

The campaign had lasted for over a decade. Crossing Afghanistan, Alexander's army suffered heavy losses. Despite the deaths, Alexander insisted that his men press on to Pakistan.

At the Hyphasis River, his men said no.

They'd suffered with Alexander, died beside Alexander, and now they were defying him. There were too many of them to execute, and he didn't want a revolt. He agreed to go back to Babylon.

Still, he tried to bring together the two very different cultures. In 324 B.C. he finally married dead King Darius's daughter, Statira. He didn't love her as he'd loved Roxane, but he believed the marriage would unite Persia and Greece. To make certain of the unity, he ordered some of his men to take Persian brides as well. He held a group ceremony including some 9,000 of their closest friends. Afterward, the party lasted for days.

Although Alexander still planned more conquests, his body ended his ambitions. Following a massive pre-battle party in late May of

This illustration depicts the funeral procession of Alexander the Great. He died on June 10 323 B.C. Alexander's empire did not survive beyond his death.

323 B.C., Alexander fell ill. Although the best doctors were called in, they could do nothing to save him.

Alexander the Great died on June 10. Some believed he was poisoned, but the most likely reason for his death was a combination of an infection, too much drinking, and poorly healed battle wounds.

The writer Arrian said that had Alexander lived, "he would never have remained idle in the enjoyment of any of his conquests, even had he extended his empire from Asia to Europe and from Europe to the British Isles."[2] His death opened the way for increasing rivalries, and the empire he'd created did not survive.

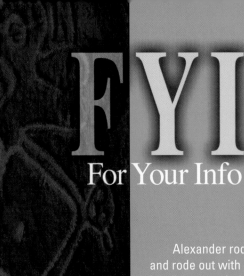

FYI
For Your Info

Afghan Power

There is a popular saying that those who don't learn the lessons of history are doomed to repeat them. Nowhere is a history lesson more valuable than in the treacherous mountains of Afghanistan. This country's geography has discouraged most invaders altogether and slowed down those who've tried.

Alexander rode into Afghanistan with a superior force of thousands and rode out with dead and wounded. The battles in Afghanistan were horrible enough that his own men almost revolted against him. It is said that some tribes in modern Afghanistan carry flags modeled after the one under which Alexander rode.

Afghans would take shelter in mountains unfamiliar to invaders and then attack at night or when their enemies were unprepared. The techniques that worked against Alexander became familiar to two 20th-century superpowers, the United States and the former Soviet Union.

In 1979, the Soviet Union invaded Afghanistan. They would leave defeated a decade later, with 15,000 of their men killed and another 50,000 wounded.

Today in Afghanistan the United States faces a similar challenge. After tying Afghan's ruling Taliban to the terrorist attacks of September 11, 2001, the United States overthrew them quickly. However, the U.S. and their allies continue to face attacks from surviving Taliban rebels who fight from the mountains.

"I feel sorry for the people who are going to be thrown into those deserted, mountainous regions where the enemy knows every single rock, every cave,"[3] Russian veteran Leo Korolkov told CNN's Jill Dougherty. "No maps, no computer training can prepare you for it."

Chronology

356 B.C.	Born on either July 20 or July 26 to Olympias and King Philip II of Macedonia
348	Alexander's formal schooling begins: tutors include Leonidas, Aristotle, and Lysimachus; tames Bucephalus
340	Is appointed Regent of Macedonia; suppresses a revolt and founds Alexandropolis; with father, expands Philip's territory
336	Alexander becomes king after his father is murdered
335	Destroys the city of Thebes following a revolution
334	Begins conquest of Asia Minor
333	Unties the Gordian knot; defeats King Darius of Persia
332	Conquers Tyre; founds city of Alexandria
331	Despite being outnumbered, his army defeats Persian army during the battle of Gaugamela
330	Takes Persepolis; becomes Great King of Persia after Darius's death
328	Marries Roxane
327	Executes leaders who plotted to overthrow him; invades India; Bucephalus dies
326	Founds the city Bucephalia in his horse's honor
324	Marries Darius's daughter Statira and forces his officers to marry other Persian women in mass wedding
323	Dies of illness compounded by unhealed battle injuries on June 10

Timeline in History

550 B.C.	Cyrus the Great Founds the Persian Empire
499-479	Persian Wars
447-432	Parthenon built in Athens as a temple to goddess Athena.
431-404	Peloponnesian War in Europe
426	Plato is born
390	Gauls attack Rome
399-362	Sparta and Thebes rule most of Greece
384	Aristotle is born
358	Philip II invades Paeonia; defeats the Illyrian king, Bardylis; invades Thessaly, and attacks the Athens-controlled city of Amphipolis
338	King Philip defeats the combined armies of the Greeks and Supreme Commander of the Greek Forces
336	Alexander the Great becomes king of Macedonia after Philip is assassinated.
335	Alexander conquers Thebes
333	Alexander defeats the army of Persia and takes control of western half of Persian Empire
331	Alexander defeats King Darius at Gaugamela and takes control of entire Persian Empire as well as all of Greece; Greek language and civilization spread to Egypt and India
326	Alexander's invasion of India ends
323	Alexander enters Babylon and dies; Ptolemy conquers Europe
300	Mayan civilization begins; Taoism develops in East Asia
264	Punic Wars begin; Carthage is destroyed
250	King Arsaces defeats Seleucid monarchy
202	Scipio Africanus defeats Hannibal at Zama
183	Death of Hannibal, who commits suicide to avoid capture by Romans

BIOGRAPHY FROM
ANCIENT CIVILIZATIONS
LEGENDS, FOLKLORE, AND STORIES OF ANCIENT WORLDS

Chapter Notes

CHAPTER ONE

1. www.eclassics.com

2. Ibid.

CHAPTER TWO

1. Alan Fildes and Joann Fletcher, *Alexander the Great: Son of the Gods* (Los Angeles: Getty Trust Publications), 2002, p. 17.

2. Ibid., p. 20.

CHAPTER THREE

1. Alan Fildes and Joann Fletcher, *Alexander the Great: Son of the Gods* (Los Angeles: Getty Trust Publications), 2002, p. 30.

2. Ibid.

CHAPTER FOUR

1. Alan Fildes and Joann Fletcher, *Alexander the Great: Son of the Gods* (Los Angeles: Getty Trust Publications), 2002, p. 31.

CHAPTER FIVE

1. Alan Fildes and Joann Fletcher, *Alexander the Great: Son of the Gods* (Los Angeles: Getty Trust Publications), 2002, p. 162.

2. Ibid.

3. www.cnn.com/2001/WORLD/europe/09/180ret.russia.terror/index.html

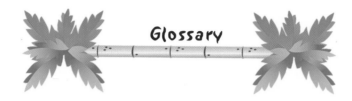

Glossary

antibiotics	(an tye BYE ah ticks)—substances produced naturally or by man that are used to fight disease-causing bacteria
catapult	(CAT ah pult)—a machine for hurling large stones and other objects
causeway	(CAWS way)—a raised roadway built over wet ground or water
cavalry	(CAH val ree)—soldiers on horseback
cholera	(COL er uh)—an often deadly disease whose symptoms include vomiting and severe muscle cramps
conspiracy	(con SPEAR ah see)—a plot involving more than one person
contemporaneous	(con tem poor AY nee us)—living at the same time
demigod	(DEM ih gahd)—a person who is more powerful than mortals but less powerful than the gods
malaria	(mah LAIR ee uh)—a disease carried by mosqui-toes that leads to chills, fever, and often death
obeisance	(oh BAY sense)—bowing or otherwise showing respect to a powerful person
oracle	(OR ah kull)—a priest or priestess believed to have the power to interpret messages from the gods
phalanx	(FAH lanx)—close formation of heavily armed troops
pharaoh	(FAIR oh)—a king in ancient Egypt
pike	a long wooden pole topped with a spear

For Further Reading

For Young Adults

Green, Robert. *Alexander the Great.* New York: Franklin Watts, 1996.

Langley, Andrew. *Alexander the Great.* New York: Oxford University Press, 1997.

Works Consulted

Connolly, Peter, and Hazel Dodge. *The Ancient City.* Oxford: Oxford University Press, 1998.

Fildes, Alan, and Joann Fletcher. *Alexander the Great: Son of the Gods.* Los Angeles: Getty Trust Publications, 2002.

Lloyd, J. G. *Alexander the Great: Selections from Arrian.* Cambridge: Cambridge University Press, 1981.

Plutarch. *Alexander "The Great," 15 Ancient Greek Heroes from Plutarch's Lives.* Abridged and annotated by Wilmot H. McCutchen at www.e-classics.com, 1998–2000.

———. *The Lives of the Noble Grecians and Romans.* Translated by John Dryden. New York: Modern Library, no copyright.

On the Internet

The Splendor of Persia
http://ali.sdc.uwo.ca/splendor3.html

The Persian Empire
http://campus.northpark.edu/history/WebChron/MiddleEast/Persia.html

Alexander the Great
http://uranus.ee.auth.gr/home/eng/Makedonia/Alexander_the_Great.html

CNN: Afghanistan, Chechnya Color Russian Terror Debate
http://www.cnn.com/2001/WORLD/europe/09/18/ret.russia.terror/index.html

Plutarch: His Life and Legacy
http://www.e-classics.com/plutarch.htm

Ask Earl: Alexander the Great
http://www.yahooligans.com/content/ask_earl/20010321.html

Index